FOREWORD BY THE 7th EARL OF DURHAM

I congratulate Andrew Jenkin on his achievement, so beautifully and romantically illustrated, and on his sensitive re-telling of the Lambton Worm legend.

I would also like to take this opportunity to extend my gratitude to my ancestors, for enduring their violent deaths in order that I might die peacefully in my bed.

Lastly, to those who may be looking for symbolic meaning to this tale, I would suggest it is a futile search, for this is simply an historically factual account of a man who killed a dragon and was cursed by a witch, in a time when such creatures actually existed, and life was more difficult and dangerous than it is now.

Ned Lambton, Earl of Durham

The Curse of the Lambton Worm

For my godsons James, Tom and Jack with love

Once upon a time, many centuries ago, there lived a noble family in a castle near the village of Lambton, in the County of Durham beside the River Wear.

The Lambton family, who were named after their village, were greatly respected throughout the land. Their youngest son, however, was regarded by everyone as a spoilt young man. This young man's name was John of Lambton.

John gave little thought for anyone and was careless of his duties, and whilst everyone else attended chapel at the nearby village of Brugeford every Sunday, he would go fishing instead.

On this particular Sunday he had caught nothing at all, and bitterly cursed the river. With that, there was a tug on the line, and he pulled with all his strength, hoping to catch what he thought was a very big fish.

Eventually he managed to reel in the thrashing creature, but this was no fish – instead, a strange black worm wriggled violently on the end of the line!

A passer-by saw what had happened and, warning him that no good would come of it, urged him to throw it back.

The day was drawing late, so the boy made his way home with the worm his only catch.

Every time he looked at the creature he was disgusted at the sight of it and eventually decided to throw it into the village well on his way home.

He walked back to the old castle and thought nothing of the horrid little worm again.

As John grew up, he began to regret his selfish youth, and eventually joined a Crusade to the Holy Land.

For seven years he fought under the fierce sun, and was recognised for his courage and determination.

The King of England learnt of his prowess and the young man was made a Knight.

Whilst he was away, however, terrible things happened in the village of Lambton.

The water in the well turned sour, and burnt the mouths and throats of anyone who drank from it.

A vile smell arose from the well, and country folk avoided the village, saying it was cursed.

Something was growing in the bottom of the well!

One morning the villagers awoke to find a trail of foul water leading from the well down to the River Wear. When they followed it, they found that a huge snake-like creature had coiled itself round a rock in the middle of the river!

Every night from then on, this strange creature roamed around the countryside, stealing lambs, sheep, and even children, and attacking cows for their milk, tearing them open with its fearsome teeth. It would sleep wrapped around a nearby hill, which people to this day call Worm Hill.

Despite attempts by the villagers to kill this monster, the giant worm grew bigger, and began to search further afield for its food, eventually making its way to the castle.

The Lord of Lambton, John's father, beside himself with fear, called his stewards to him and asked what they could do to help the village and protect the castle.

It was well-known that the creature's favourite food was milk, so in desperation a stone trough was filled to the brim with the milk of nine cows.

For a time this appeased the creature, but if anyone took as much as a cupful from its trough it seemed to know, and would rampage around the village uprooting trees and killing livestock.

Many brave knights travelled to the village and lost their lives in an attempt to kill the creature, their bones left scattered around the Worm Hill.

When John of Lambton, now Sir John, Knight of Rhodes, returned home, he found the villagers in a state of terror and his father desperate for a solution.

The villagers told the knight about the terrible worm; he listened to their pleas and was determined to help them if he could.

That evening the villagers led Sir John to the Worm Hill, where he saw the monstrous beast for himself. It was a hideous snake-like creature, its bulging body wrapped three times around the hill.

In horror, the knight realised that this was the same creature that he had fished from the River Wear so many years before! Full of remorse for blighting his land with such a terrible curse, Sir John knew that it was now up to him to find some way of making amends.

In nearby Brugeford there lived an old woman, whom some called a witch. She was a wise woman, who made herbal potions to heal or harm, and would talk to the creatures around her. Aware of her reputation, Sir John went to her for advice.

As soon as the witch saw him she knew that it was he who had caught this repulsive creature and brought sorrow upon his people, and that only he would be able to kill the Worm.

The witch told the knight that the worm would try to kill him by coiling itself around him so tightly that he would suffocate and be crushed to death.

She warned him that if he chopped the worm to pieces, as the brave knights had tried before him, the pieces would re-join, and the worm would become whole again.

She told him that the only way to kill the worm was for its head to be struck off so that it could not re-join its body.

Whispering, she told him a way in which this might be done, but she uttered a clear warning along with her advice …

The witch warned Sir John that he must vow to kill the first living creature that he set eyes upon, once he had slain the Worm, or his family would be cursed, and for nine generations no Lord of Lambton would die peacefully in his bed.

Taking heed of her warning and advice, the knight thanked the old woman and set off back to the village.

Sir John instructed the village blacksmith to fashion a suit of armour strong enough to withstand great pressure, and covered in long sharp spikes.

He told his father's servants that, on hearing a blast from his hunting horn, they must release his most faithful hound at once. He knew that this would be the first living creature that he saw, so he could fulfil his vow.

He left strict instructions that no-one was to venture near the river until they had heard a second blast from his horn.

Clad in his new armour, brave Sir John, Knight of Rhodes, made his way to the chapel at Brugeford to make his vow, then rode down to the River Wear to face the dragon.

The Worm, basking in the sunshine on its rock in the middle of the river, opened one glassy eye and lazily flicked its tongue to taste the air. An evil smell issued from its breath. Calmly, the knight dismounted and sent his horse away, then waded into the middle of the fast-flowing river. Drawing his sword, he resolutely turned to face the vile creature.

The Worm slowly uncoiled itself from the rock and slid into the water.

Circling in the water around him, the Worm drew nearer and nearer, rearing above him, until its huge slavering mouth was all Sir John could see. It began to wrap its coils around the slow-moving knight, intending to smother him, but the knight's heavy armour held firm and did not bend or buckle.

Entwined and fighting for breath amidst the bulging and heaving mass, Sir John was engulfed with fear.

The monster squeezed him harder and harder, but as it pressed, the spikes on the armour began to pierce through the Worm's thick scales, tearing its belly to shreds.

Slowly, as the fleshy strips were torn away, they floated down the river in thick bloody lumps, unable to re-join the body. Bleeding and exhausted, the worm finally loosened its hold on Sir John, and tried to heave itself out of the river and return to its hill.
Drawing on all his remaining strength, the knight raised his sword high, and lopped off the worm's head with one mighty blow.

The worm's eyes rolled, its body writhing at the water's edge. Carried by the river, the remains of the huge body drifted away, leaving only the lifeless head on the river bank.

The knight fell to the ground, and silence descended

Eventually he raised his hunting horn and gave a triumphant blast to tell the servants to release the hound. His father, however, was so overjoyed to know that his son had survived, that he forgot his son's instructions, and rushed out of the castle to meet him before the servants had time to release the hound.

Expecting to see the hound come running to the river, Sir John looked on in horror as he watched his own father come bounding down the hill towards him, waving his arms and shouting with relief.

Too late, the knight's faithful dog followed him.

Despite having to break his vow, the knight could not bring himself to kill his own father, and slew the hound instead, but he knew this would not prevent the curse on his family.

He and his jubilant father rode back to the castle amidst the cheers of the thronging villagers, who were so happy that they did not notice the knight's sorrow.

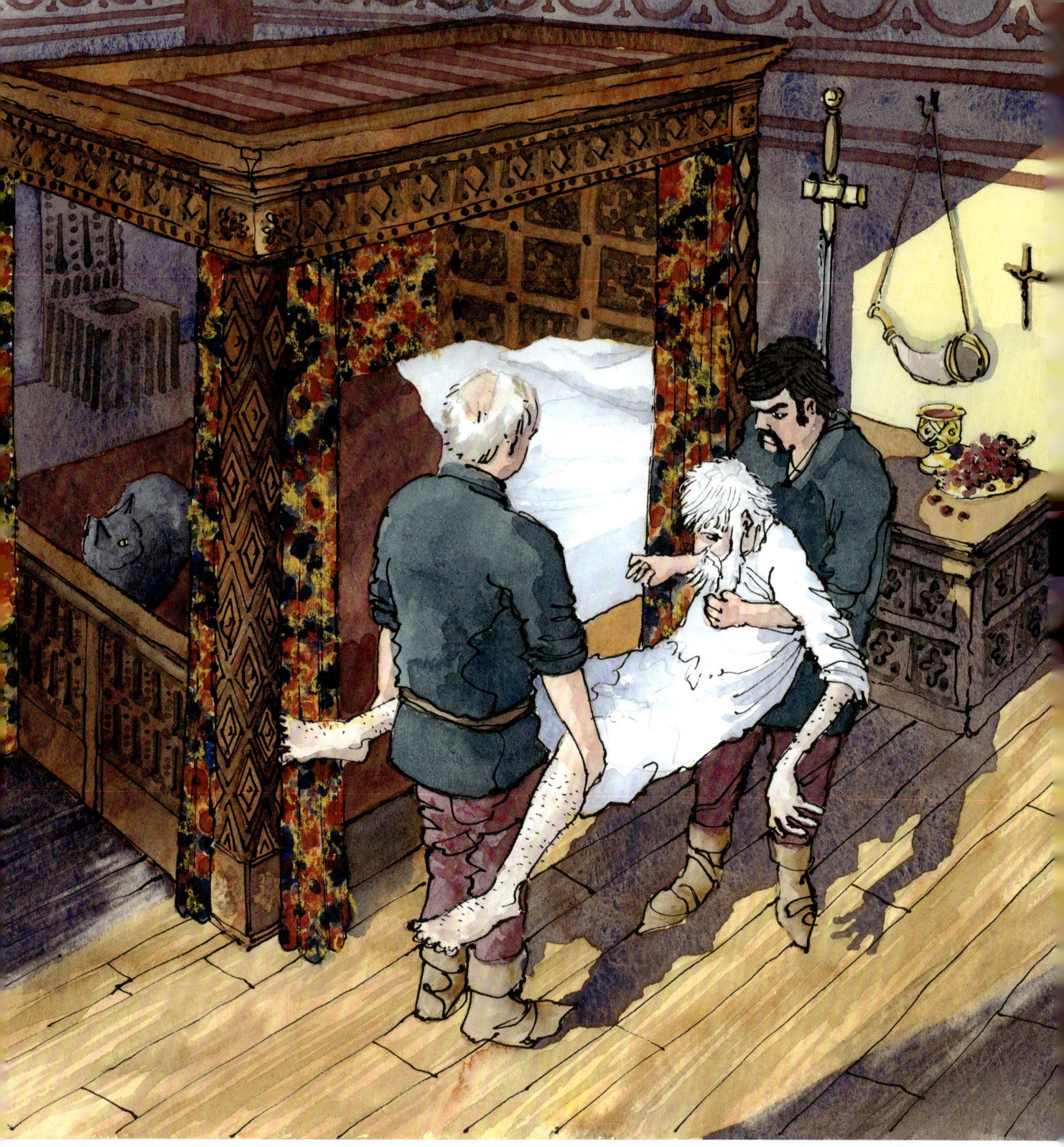

Telling no-one else of the curse, Sir John lived for many years; his family prospered and he became a lord of the realm. In time though, he became so old and weak that he was eventually bed-ridden.

It was then that he told people of the curse, and only when his servants lifted him from his bed could he finally die, but the curse had only just begun.

For nine generations, the lords of Lambton would not die peacefully in their beds.

Sir John's own son was drowned in the river near the chapel of Brugeford.

His descendants were strangled and stabbed, throttled and skewered ... those few who died peacefully, died in foreign lands, far from home.

The ninth lord died crossing a bridge over the River Wear, not far from where young John had caught the worm centuries before.

With his death the curse of the Lambton Worm finally ended.

BACKGROUND TO THE STORY

The name Worm comes from the old Norse word for dragon, 'Orm' and from the Anglo Saxon word 'Wyrm' meaning serpent or dragon. Worm legends are particularly plentiful in the north-east of England, and the legends of the Laidley Worm of Bamburgh, and the Sockburn Worm near Darlington bear great similarity to the Lambton Worm legend.

It has been suggested that such legends may have some allegorical meaning, representing a conflict of some kind, or are simply morality tales. Some historians writing in the 18th and 19th centuries, such as Durham historian William Hutchinson, believed that they could have been a representation of an invasion by a foreign foe and that the Worm may have symbolised Viking invaders whose longships bore a prominent dragon's head. The north-east was raided by the Vikings during the Dark Ages (5th – 11th century).

It is equally possible that the earlier legends refer to the 'Harrying of the North' which occurred soon after the Norman Conquest in the 11th century when William the Conqueror sent his army north to York and Durham, with the intention of replacing the Anglo-Scandinavian lords with his Norman ones, and was met with fierce resistance.

The Lambton Worm legend however, refers to a much later period – probably the late 14th or early 15th century. Durham historian Robert Surtees suggested that this legend could refer to the regular invasions by the Scots. He suggests that the enemy's advance in line over uneven ground would appear to the frightened peasants as a rolling serpent, and the power of re-uniting would represent military tactics of an army re-forming. The invader would naturally encamp on an eminence for better security – Worm Hill? – and the knight in the legend could have been the leader of the defenders, whilst the severing of the body might imply the tactics of cutting off groups of soldiers from the main army.

A much more down-to-earth explanation could be that the legend began as a moral cautionary tale, to dissuade those who decided to neglect their Sunday worship, or even to protect the fishing rights on the Lambton Hall estate!

A 14th century legend from Rhodes tells of a fierce dragon, which having killed several knights, was finally slain by the young Knight of Rhodes, Dieudonné de Goza. He devised a plan to kill it with the aid of trained dogs, and his gravestone read 'Here lies the dragon slayer'. Sir John Lambton, as a Knight of Rhodes himself, would have been fully aware of this legend and would no doubt have recounted the story on his return to England. Could this be where the legend originated?

The idea that there really was a huge fearsome creature, however, cannot be dismissed. We only have to look at the continuing modern-day beliefs in and sightings of the Loch Ness Monster, to realise the strength of conviction that would have been felt. Certainly the romantic poets and novelists such as Sir Walter Scott, and Victorian scientists and historians, such as William Hylton Longstaffe, believed that there could have been a large serpent-like creature still in existence in certain country areas. Much of the belief in giant reptiles would have been reinforced by the fossils of dinosaurs which have been found in abundance along the north-east coast for several centuries. John Walbran, the 19th century historian, also believed that the legends could really have been about reptiles, but their size may have been 'magnified and misrepresented in their transmission through centuries by the ignorance of the narrators'.

Even in the nineteenth century, historians Robert Surtees and Eneas Mackenzie described much of the area as consisting of wide deep fast-flowing rivers, with deep overhanging banks and dense tangled woodland and marshy shrubland, which could have harboured some overgrown creature which terrorised the district, but this may have been a huge wild boar or wolf and the true facts became altered and exaggerated..

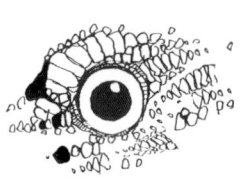

The story of the Lambton Worm is probably the north-east of England's most well-known legend, which was passed down as oral tradition for centuries in the area. There appears to be no published account of the legend prior to the early 19th century, and the original publication of the legend can be attributed to the Durham historian Robert Surtees (1779 – 1834), who began research for a four-volume work on the history of Durham in 1804. Surtees dedicated much of his life to recording local history and superstition as accurately as possible, corroborating his evidence wherever he could.

Many versions of the Lambton legend and accompanying historical commentaries have since been published, but they are all based on that by Robert Surtees. Some later versions of the legend describe the Lambton Worm as a creature with a salamander-like head and nine holes on either side of its mouth; the salamander is unique amongst vertebrates in that it can regenerate lost limbs and other body parts, in the same way that the Worm's body rejoins in the legend. If we are to take Surtees' account as the definitive version, he merely describes the young Worm as a "small worm or eft" (young eel) and the description may have become embellished over the years. This re-telling keeps fairly close to the Surtees version of the tale, with a few exceptions - in Surtees' version, Sir John Lambton had several attempts at killing the Worm before he was successful, and his armour was embedded with razor blades rather than spear-heads. Surtees noted that versions of the oral tradition differed over whether it was young John Lambton himself who actually caught the worm and threw it in the well, or whether it was some unknown miscreant.

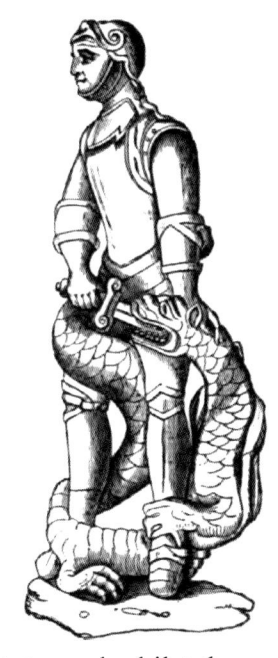

Surtees was familiar with the story of the Lambton Worm from childhood, and recalled as a boy "having seen something exhibited in old Lambton Hall that was a part of the Worm's skin, like a piece of tough bull's hide, and a real good Andrea Ferrara [a good quality sword] inscribed on the blade 1521 - notwithstanding the date – is said to be the identical weapon by which the worm perished". He also remembered seeing the stone trough from which the Worm was reputed to have drunk the milk of nine cows at the Hall. It is unknown where these artefacts are now.

Two statues, which are reputed to date from the early 1600's, once stood at Lambton Hall. One depicts a woman thought to be the wise woman; the other statue depicts a knight slaying the Lambton Worm, with the back of his armour inlaid with razor blades; his left hand is holding the head of the worm, and with his right he appears to be thrusting his sword into its throat. An early drawing of this (shown right) appeared in 'The Bishoprick Garland' by Sir Cuthbert Sharpe and Andrew was kindly given permission to view the statues which are still in the possession of the Lambton family.

Surtees stayed regularly with friends in Herrington, not far from the Lambton estate, and whilst there, met local historian Elizabeth Cockburn of nearby Offerton, who recounted the traditional version of the legend, which he included in the second volume of his work 'History and Antiquities of the County Palatine of Durham' published in 1820.

According to letters written by Sir John George Lambton, later 1st Earl of Durham (which are included in a book 'Memoirs of Robert Surtees' by George Taylor & others) we know that Surtees consulted him during his research on the history of Chester-le-Street and the Lambton Worm legend. The correspondence shows that Sir John George Lambton read and corrected the draft version of the book and in February 1819 returned it with a note "I have also marked several passages in the History of the Lambton Worm tradition which either do not tally with the tradition as given in my family, or which seem to me savouring a little too much of 'persiflage' [frivolousness]"; so we know that Surtees published the version of the Lambton Worm legend with the authority of the Lambton family.

In other correspondence in March 1819 Surtees asked Sir John George Lambton for his view on the origin of the legend of the Lambton Worm, to which Lambton replied "I really cannot comply with your request of stating what my idea of the Worm tradition is. It is impossible to come at the truth of that description. The only result I draw is, that one of my family rendered some service or other to the county by some action which has come down to us in the guise of the Worm". So we too can only speculate, and should perhaps take the advice of the present Earl of Durham given in the foreword to this book!

The Lambton Family

The intriguing thing about the Legend of the Lambton Worm, is that not only does it refer to a real family and we can even trace the 'dragon-slayer' in the family tree, but it also refers to real places which we can still trace today. The Lambton family is still prestigious, and the current Lord of Lambton is the Hon. Frederick Lambton, son of Ned Lambton, the 7th Earl of Durham. The Lambtons (originally spelt Lamtun) can trace their origins in County Durham to at least the early 12th century, and take their name from the local village of the same name. The first recorded member of the Lambton family was John de Lamtun in 1180, who was witness to a Charter of Uchtred de Wodeshend on the nearby Lumley estate, but it was a later family member, Sir John Lambton, Knight of Rhodes (a religious military order established in 1309), who is believed to have slain the legendary Lambton Worm.

This Sir John appears in the Lambton family tree - his father was called William, and his mother Elizabeth. He had three elder brothers Robert, Thomas and William, and two sisters Alice and Elizabeth. In his brother Robert's will in 1442 he is named as 'Sir John, Knight of Rhodes ', and he is similarly named, along with his sisters in his mother's will of 1439. Robert Surtees refers to an ancient manuscript which was in the possession of the Middleton family of Offerton, which states 'Johan Lambeton that slewe ye Worme was Knight of Rhoodes and Lord of Lambton and Wod Apilton, after the dethe [*death*] of fower [*four*] brothers sans esshewe masle [*without male children*]. His son Robert Lampton [sic] was drowned at Newebrigg'. John could not have inherited the title of Lord of Lambton, however, until after 1474 when the third of his older brothers died, but it was Thomas, the eldest, whose line continued the Lambton pedigree.

The Lambton Curse

According to popular tradition, for nine generations the Lords of Lambton did not die in their own beds. There does not appear to be any written evidence to support whether the 'curse' affected each of the nine generations, and it may only have been remarked on when a tragedy occurred within the family, and people blamed it on the curse! Below are listed the family members (taken from various Victorian history books and an article in the Chicago Times from 1928) who are alleged to have died untimely deaths:

- Sir John's son, Robert Lambton, is reputed to have drowned at New Bridge, near to the chapel at Brugeford.
- Sir Ralph Lambton was condemned to death by Henry VIII as a Papist and was beheaded.
- The Venerable Joseph Lambton, second son of Thomas Lambton of Malton in Rydall and his wife Katherine Byrkett, was executed by Queen Elizabeth I on 24th July 1592 in Newcastle for being a Catholic priest.
- Sir Roger Lambton was reputedly shot by a highwayman in 1628. His brothers John and William died in the same year of unknown causes.
- John Lambton, son of Ralph from the Tribley branch of the Lambton family, was killed during the English Civil War in a skirmish at Bradford on 20th May 1643.
- Sir William Lambton, a Royalist and Colonel of a regiment of Foot in the service of Charles I, was killed at the Battle of Marston Moor in 1644.
- William Lambton (Sir William's eldest son by his second wife) who was Captain of Horse in the service of Charles I received head wounds and died at the Battle at Wakefield in 1643, where he was at the head of a troop of dragoons.
- William's brother Sir Thomas Lambton, was Colonel of all Horse in the Bishopric of Durham, and was killed at the Battle of Sedgefield in 1662.
- On June 26th 1761 Sir Henry Lambton died in his carriage crossing Lambton Bridge. By tradition, this was the generation with whom the curse would end, but despite this, his brother John, a Major-General, who lived to a great age, was reputed to have kept a horse-whip beside him during his last illness, in fear that his servants might try to continue the prophecy!
- It is exactly nine generations ascending from Henry Lambton with whom the curse was said to end, to Sir John Lambton, Knight of Rhodes who slew the worm.

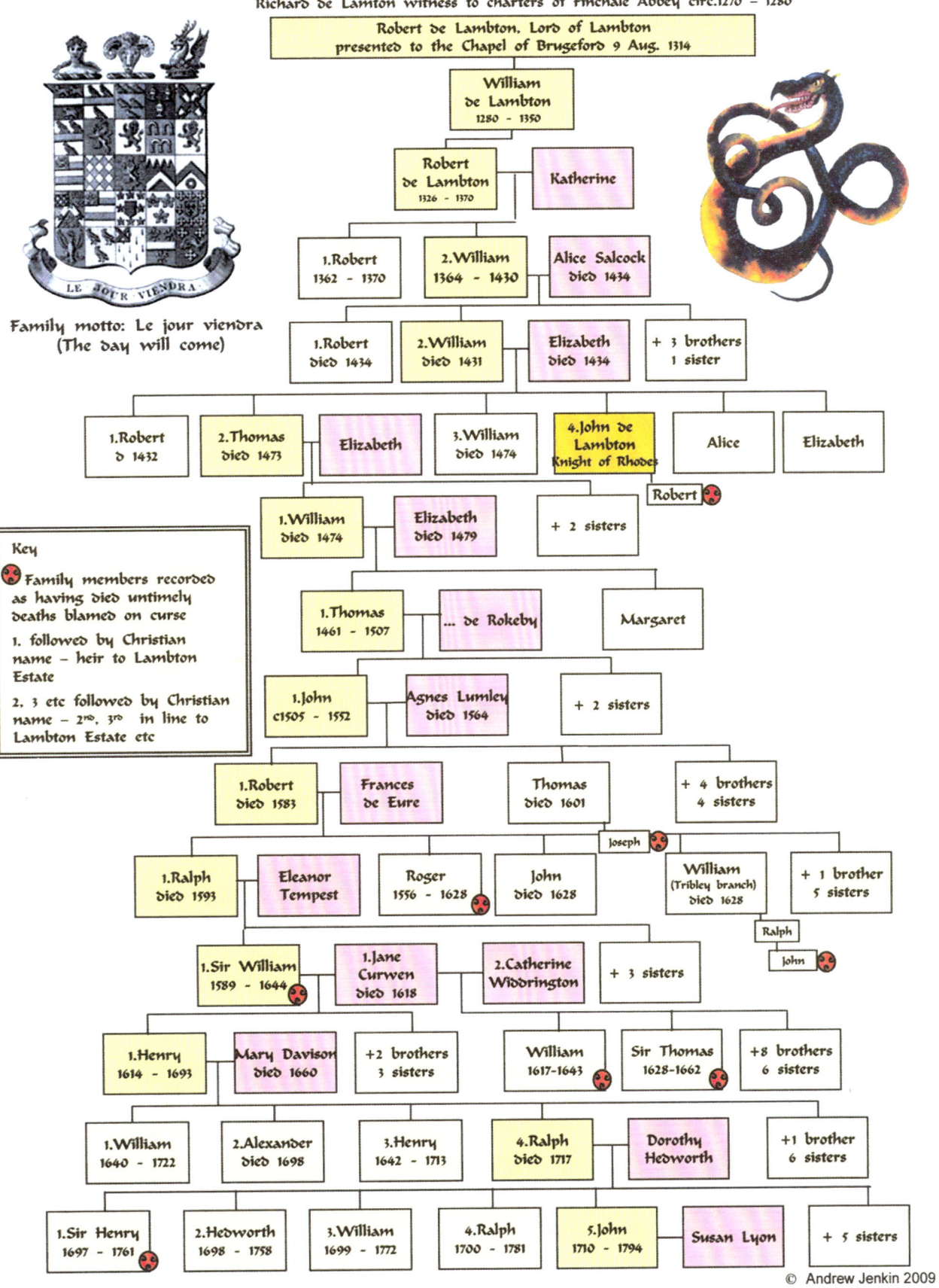

The family tree shows Sir John Lambton and the descending nine generations who were allegedly 'cursed!'

The locations

The village of Lambton was first recorded in 1421; the name comes from the Old English words Lam Tun - 'the enclosure where the lambs are kept'. The modern village of Lambton lies to the east of Chester-le-Street close to the A19 and is a district of Washington new town.

The original home of the Lambtons was a manor house, northwest of Bournmoor on the south side of the River Wear; this would have been the home of Sir John Lambton in the legend. In the 16th century the family built **Lambton Hall** (private land) on the same site, which was demolished in 1797 when they commissioned the building of a much grander Lambton Castle. All that remains of Lambton Hall now are the old Brewery Cottages - parts of the walls and two of the round quatrefoil windows on the front were converted from the remains of the Hall. Robert Surtees described the Hall as "a double house with flanking gavel-ended wings, and the grounds laid out in parterres and terraces".

SKETCH MAP SHOWING LOCATIONS ASSOCIATED WITH THE LAMBTON WORM

N.B. Some locations are on private land

The later 18th century **Lambton Castle** (private land) was built on the core of the earlier Harraton Hall on the north side of the river and stands in extensive private parkland, the Lambton Park Estate. In the 1930's the family moved to the smaller stately Biddick Hall (private land), an early 18th century house at the park's eastern end. Lambton Castle has sometimes been confused with the much older Lumley Castle (Grid ref NZ2287510) to the south across the river near Chester-le-Street. This was built in the 14th century, and in the 1500's, a John Lambton married Agnes Lumley of Ludworth (a great-granddaughter of Edward IV), thus forming a link between the Lumleys and the Lambtons.

The River Wear flows through the Lambton estate as it does in the legend, and the site of **Brugeford** or Bridgeford, where the legendary "wise woman of Brugeford" lived, is by Chester New Bridge which crosses the Wear beside the A183 (Grid ref NZ284522) near Chester-le-Street. This medieval bridge was first mentioned in 1528 as 'Newbrigge'.

Brugeford Chapel was reputedly the chapel which the young John of Lambton forsook for his fishing on that fateful day, and in which he later swore his vow. It is thought to have been built in the 1100's if not before, and it is recorded that the Lambton family worshipped there from before 1200 until the time of Henry VIII when it fell into disuse. The chapel no longer exists, but the historian Hutchinson described it in 1785: "At a farmhouse leading to Lambton are the remains of a chapel, the stonework of the eastern window yet perfect, and in the front of the house in a circle, is the figure of a man to the waist, in relief, with elevated hands …. its location was near the New Bridge on the left of the road immediately within the entrance of Lambton Park".

This drawing of the ruined chapel at Brugeford is reproduced from "The Bishoprick Garland" by Sir Cuthbert Sharpe, 1834.

The chapel is said to have been demolished in 1797 at the same time as Lambton Hall.

Worm Well (Grid ref NZ311540) is just south of Worm Hill, past The Biddick Inn down Bonemill Lane. The Victorian historian Robert Surtees describes the Worm Well as situated between Worm Hill and the River Wear, 26 yards from the hill, 48 yards from the river. Worm Well was reputed to be a wishing well in the mid-18th century, and was used during festivities on Midsummer's Eve. Originally the well had a lid and an iron dish or ladle.

Women would drop bent pins down it as an offering to the fairies - this was an old superstition which held that the fairies needed the pins to make tiny arrow-heads for hunting, and would in return reveal the identity of the person's future husband by letting them see his reflection in the water of the well.

By the time the historian Hewitt visited the well in 1842 it had 'vanished entirely, being drained into the river'. The Worm Well that exists now resembles a stone trough rather than a well, and the water seems to flow into it from Worm Hill.

Worm Hill (Grid ref NZ310540) is located opposite Worm Hill Terrace, Fatfield near Washington, on the north side of the Wear, about a mile and a half from the old Lambton Hall. It was most likely formed from a type of glacial moraine called a kame, and is tear-drop in shape and smooth-sided, but according to historians such as Stephen Oliver, furrows formed by the worm as it lay coiled round the hill still existed when he was writing in 1835.

Penshaw Hill (Grid ref NZ335543), a mile to the east, is often confused with Worm Hill as being the lair of the Lambton Worm. Penshaw is the site of the only Iron Age hillfort with triple ramparts in the north-east of England, and the spiral furrows formed by the ramparts might well have given rise to speculation about a dragon coiling itself three times round the hill. Penshaw Hill is actually connected with a much later member of the Lambton family – John George Lambton, first Earl of Durham and Governor General of Canada (1792-1840), known to Durham pitmen as 'Radical Jack' because of the political reforms he instigated in the 19th century. Penshaw Monument, built in the style of a Greek temple on top of Penshaw Hill, was built in 1844 in memory of the Earl.

Worm Hill, Fatfield with Worm Hill Terrace and Penshaw Hill in the background

Much of the enduring fame of the Lambton Worm is owed to the song which was written for the pantomime version of 'The Lambton Worm' in 1867 by C.M.Leumane, and which has been adopted as a folk song. The pantomime was first performed at Tyne Theatre and Opera House in Newcastle-upon-Tyne. The lyrics and music are printed at the front of this book.

An earlier ballad about the Lambton Worm was written by the Rev J.Watson in the mid-1800's called 'The Worme of Lambton', and was about one hundred stanzas long. It was first published in 'Tait's Edinburgh Magazine' and later appeared in a book, 'The Local Historian's Table-book', with evidence said to have been gleaned from live accounts from elderly people in the area – these accounts are actually the same as those presented by Robert Surtees, the historian, a few years earlier.

The legend's popularity continued, and in 1978 an opera was published entitled 'The Lambton Worm'. This opera in two acts, was composed by Robert Sherlaw Johnson with libretto (words) by the Oxford poet Anne Ridler.

The novel 'The Lair of the White Worm', written by Bram Stoker in 1911, was based loosely on the legend, with the hero named 'John Dampton'; this was made into a film by Ken Russell in 1988. Bram Stoker, who also wrote 'Dracula', was manager of the Lyceum Theatre in Sunderland for many years, so had close association with the district.

The famous poem 'The Jabberwocky' was written during Lewis Carroll's stay with relatives at Whitburn, near Sunderland, although the first stanza was written in Croft-on-Tees, close to nearby Darlington, where Carroll lived as a boy. He was probably already aware of the legend of the Sockburn Worm, and it is thought that the legend of the Lambton Worm may also have been an inspiration to him.

The popularity of the legend has continued throughout the Sunderland, Durham and Newcastle area, and the Lambton Worm is often featured in festivals and celebrations, or used as a symbol representing the area, helping to keep the legend alive.

For example, in 1984 Robert Olley was commissioned to design an animated Lambton Worm clock for the new shopping centre 'The Galleries' in Washington new town. The 17-foot high fibre-glass castle was suspended from the roof, and cartoon figures of Lord Lambton holding the severed head of the Worm, and several other characters from the legend rotated around it when the clock struck the hour. This was a popular attraction and remained in place until 1990 when it was dismantled and is now in storage.